THE GATES

McGRAW-HILL BOOK COMPANY

New York • St. Louis • San Francisco
Düsseldorf • Mexico • Toronto

THE GATES

Poems by Muriel Rukeyser

*Some of the poems in this book have appeared in
the following publications:* American Poetry Review,
American Writing, American Scholar, Antaeus, Black Box, Lilith,
Ms., Neruda Reader, Ontario Review, Writers and Teachers Magazine.
To these publications and to their editors, my thanks.

Book design by Lynn Braswell

123456789   BPBP   79876

Library of Congress Cataloging in Publication Data

Rukeyser, Muriel, 1913–
   The gates : poems.

   I. Title.
PS3535.U4G3   811'.5'2   76-20738
ISBN 0–07–054268–6
ISBN 0–07–054269–4 pbk.

For Jacob & Kang
& the future

CONTENTS

TWO ·81·

ONE

ST. ROACH

For that I never knew you, I only learned to dread you,
for that I never touched you, they told me you are filth,
they showed me by every action to despise your kind;
for that I saw my people making war on you,
I could not tell you apart, one from another,
for that in childhood I lived in places clear of you,
for that all the people I knew met you by
crushing you, stamping you to death, they poured boiling
    water on you, they flushed you down,
for that I could not tell one from another
only that you were dark, fast on your feet, and slender.
    Not like me.
For that I did not know your poems
And that I do not know any of your sayings
And that I cannot speak or read your language
And that I do not sing your songs
And that I do not teach our children
              to eat your food
              or know your poems
              or sing your songs
But that we say you are filthing our food
But that we know you not at all.

Yesterday I looked at one of you for the first time.
You were lighter than the others in color, that was
    neither good nor bad.

I was really looking for the first time.
You seemed troubled and witty.

Today I touched one of you for the first time.
You were startled, you ran, you fled away
Fast as a dancer, light, strange and lovely to the touch.
I reach, I touch, I begin to know you.

DREAM-DRUMMING

I braced the drum to my arm, a flat drum, and began to
   play.
He heard me and she heard me. I had never seen this
   drum before.
As I played, weakness went through me; weakness left me.
      I held my arms high, the drum and the soft-headed
         long stick
I drummed past my tiredness vibrating weakness, past
   it into music,
As in ragas past exhaustion into the country of all music.

Held my arms high, became that vibration, drummed the
   sacrifice of my belly.
He heard me, she heard me,
I turned into the infinity figure, reaching down into
   the earth of music with my legs at last,
Reaching up from the two circles, my pelvic sea,
   mountains and air of breast, with my arms up into
      music
At last turned into music, drumming on that possessed
   vibration,
Drumming my dream.

DOUBLE ODE

for Bill & Alison

I

Wine and oil gleaming within their heads,
I poured it into the hollow of their bodies
but they did not speak.   The light glittered.
Lit from underneath they were.   Water
pouring over her face, it
made the lips move and the eyes move, she
spoke:
Break open.
He did not speak.
A still lake shining in his head,
until I knew that the sun and the moon
stood in me with one light.

II

They began to breathe and glitter.   Morning
overflowed, gifts poured from their sex
upon my throat and my breast.
They knew.   They laughed.   In their tremendous games
night revolved and shook my bed.   I
woke in a cold morning.
Your presences
allow me to begin to make myself
carried on your shoulders, swayed in your arms.
Something is flashing among the colors.   I
move without being allowed.   I

move with the blessing of the sky and the sea.

III

Tonight I will try again for the music of truth
since this one and that one of mine are met with death.
It is a blind lottery, a cheap military trumpet
with all these great roots black under the earth
while a muscle-legged man
stamps in his red and gold
rough wine, creatures in nets, swords through their spines
and all their cantillation in our thought.

Glitter and pedestal under my female powers
a woman singing horses, blind cities of concrete, moon
comes to moonrise as a dark daughter.
I am the poet of the night of women
and my two parents are the sun and the moon,
a strong father of that black double likeness,
a bell kicking out of the bell-tower,
and a mother who shines and shines his light.

Who is the double ghost whose head is smoke?
Her thighs hold the wild infant, a trampled country
and I will fly in, in all my fears.
Those two have terrified me, but I live,
their silvery line of music gave me girlhood
and fierce male prowess and a woman's grave
eternal double music male and female,
inevitable blue, repeated evening

of the two.   Of the two.

IV

But these two figures are not the statues east and west
at my long window on the river they are mother and
    father
but not my actual parents only their memory.
Not memory but something builded in my cells

Father with your feet cut off
mother cut down to death
cut down my sister in the selfsame way
and my abandoned husband a madman of the sun
and you dark outlaw the other one when do we speak
The song flies out of all of you the song
starts in my body, the song
it is in my mouth, the song
it is on my teeth, the song
it is pouring the song
wine and lightning
the rivers coming to confluence
in me entire.

V

But that was years ago.   My child is grown.
His wife and he in exile, that is, home,
longing for home, and I home, that is exile, the much-
    loved country

like the country called parents, much-loved that was, and
    exile.
His wife and he turning toward the thought
of their own child, conceive we say, a child.
Now rise in me the old dealings : father, mother,
not years ago, but in my last-night dream,
waking this morning, the two Mexican figures
black stone with their stone hollows I fill with water,
fill with wine, with oil, poems and lightning.
Black in morning dark, the sky going blue,
the river going blue.

Moving toward new form I am—
carry again
all the old gifts and wars.

VI

Black parental mysteries
groan and mingle in the night.
Something will be born of this.

Pay attention to what they tell you to forget
pay attention to what they tell you to forget
pay attention to what they tell you to forget

Farewell the madness of the guardians
the river, the window, they are the guardians,
there is no guardian, it is all built into me.

Do I move toward form, do I use all my fears?

PAINTERS

In the cave with a long-ago flare
a woman stands, her arm up. Red twig, black twig, brown
    twig.
A wall of leaping darkness over her.
The men are out hunting in the early light
But here in this flicker, one or two men, painting
and a woman among them.
Great living animals grow on the stone walls,
their pelts, their eyes, their sex, their hearts,
and the cave-painters touch them with life, red, brown,
    black,
a woman among them, painting.

RUNE

The word in the bread feeds me,
The word in the moon leads me,
The word in the seed breeds me,
The word in the child needs me.

The word in the sand builds me,
The word in the fruit fills me,
The word in the body mills me,
The word in the war kills me.

The word in the man takes me,
The word in the storm shakes me,
The word in the work makes me,
The word in the woman rakes me,
The word in the word wakes me.

HOW WE DID IT

We all traveled into that big room,
some from very far away
we smiled at some we knew
we did not as we talked agree
our hearts went fast thinking of morning
when we would walk along the path.
We spoke.   Late night.   We disagreed.
We knew we would climb the Senate steps.
We knew we would present our claim
we would demand : be strong now : end the war.
How would we do it?   What would we ask?
"We will be warned," one said. "They will warn us and
    take us."
"We can speak and walk away."
"We can lie down as if in mourning."
"We can lie down as a way of speech,
speaking of all the dead in Asia."
Then Eqbal said, "We are not at this moment
a revolutionary group, we are
a group of dissenters.   Let some, then,
walk away, let some stand until they want to leave,
let some lie down and let some be arrested.   Some of us.
Let each do what he feels at that moment
tomorrow."   Eqbal's dark face.
The doctor spoke, of friendships made in jail.

We looked into each other's eyes
and went all to our rooms, to sleep,
waiting for morning.

ISLANDS

O for God's sake
they are connected
underneath

They look at each other
across the glittering sea
some keep a low profile

Some are cliffs
The bathers think
islands are separate like them

BLUE SPRUCE

Of all green trees, I love a nevergreen
blue among dark blue, these almost black
needles guarded the door there was, years
before the white guardians over Sète
. . . that's Sea France at the Sea Cemetery
near Spain where Valéry . . .
those short square Mediterranean
man and woman
couple at the black-cut shadow door
within the immense marine
glare of noon,
and on the beach
leaning from one strong hip
a bearded Poseidon
looking along the surface of the sea
father and husband there he stands
and an invisible woman him beside
blue-eyed blue-haired blue-shadowed
under the sun and the moon
they blaze upon us
and we waiting waiting
swim to the source
very blue evening now deepening
needles of light ever new
a tree of light and a tree of darkness
blue spruce

ARTIFACT

When this hand is gone to earth,
this writing hand and the paper beneath it,
long gone, and the words on the paper forgotten,
and the breath that slowly curls around earth with
                        its old spoken words
gone into lives unborn and they too gone to earth—
and their memory, memory of any of these gone,
and all who remembered them absorbed in air and dirt,
words, earth, breeze over the oceans, all these now other,
there may as in the past be something left,
some artifact. This pen. Will it tell my? Will it tell
   our?
This thing made in bright metal by thousands unknown
   to me,
will it arrive with that unnameable wish to speak a music,
offering something out of all I moved among?
singing for others unknown a long-gone moment in old
   time sung?

                            The pen—
will some broken pieces be assembled by women, by guess-
   ing men
(or future mutations, beings unnamed by us)—
can these dry pieces join? Again go bright? Speak to you
   then?

MS. LOT

Well, if he treats me like a young girl still,
That father of mine, and here's my sister
And we're still traveling into the hills—
But everyone on the road knows he offered us
To the Strangers when all they wanted was men,
And the cloud of smoke still over the twin cities
And mother a salt lick the animals come to—
Who's going to want me now?
Mother did not even know
She was not to turn around and look.
God spoke to Lot, my father.
She was hard of hearing.   He knew that.
I don't believe he told her, anyway.
What kind of father is that, or husband?
He offered us to those men.   They didn't want women.
Mother always used to say:
Some normal man will come along and need you.

BOYS IN THE BRANCHES

Blue in the green trees, what are they climbing?
And girls bringing water, what are they watering
With their buckets spilling the wet dark on dry ground?

And up the hill the concrete-mixers rolling
Owned by my father when I was the same youth
As these who are my students, boys in the branches,
Young women in the young trees.

The last few drops from the faucet, carried
To the tan crumbling earth.
The earth belongs to the authorities
Of this college, and the authorities
Have turned the water off, have they?

Ask the owners of colleges, who is in the trees?
Ask the owners of concrete-mixers, who is holding
This acre of city land against the concrete?
We know where the water is.

Blue green students in the branches
Defending the tree.   The trees begin to shudder.
The concrete-mixers roll over exposed roots.

But isn't all this a romantic delusion?
You love the pouring of the city, don't you?

You need the buildings, don't you?
Sift the seeds.   We need to sift the seeds.

We know where the water is.
They have turned the water off.
You don't want buildings not to be built, do you?
The blueprint lies on the flat-top desk.

The building now is two years built,
Most of the boys went off to war,
I don't teach there any more.

Here we go, swimming to civilization,
We who stand and water and sift the seeds,
My students saying their word, it flies behind what I hear
    in the air:
"Time is God's blood," Warren said.   Avra wrote:
"Forgive me, Mother. I am alive."

SONG : LYING IN DAYLIGHT

Lying in daylight, in the strong
light of all our fantasies,
now touch speaking to touch, touch sees—
night and light, the darkness-stare,
your long look that pierces where
light never came till now—
moving is what we do,
moving we are, searching,
going high and underground,
rain behind rain pouring down,
river under river going
silence on silence
sound under sound.

HYPNOGOGIC FIGURE

In woods you know stands the wonder-working madonna
You stub your foot on the plinth when you walk lost
    among trees
She looks like your small bronze bell, the one in the
    shape of
a little girl with a stand-up collar
But it is limitless and dark, of tarnished silver
When you crawl under her skirt, you will see the inside
but up there, the clapper is gone, nothing is hanging down;
bulging like Atreus' treasure-chamber, a great bell
Ask for her sons, there are many, X, Y and Z
You may find a door in the creases of underwear
and grope your way up along peculiar stairways
winding in precarious spirals like the climb up the tower
    at Pisa
You are dizzy already. The risers are irregular
Gravity works against the spiral and the balance
you thought built-in no longer functions, you stumble
Above the vault is her waist, you see it as her belt
from the inside, a shimmer of colors, yellow violet and
    blood-red
It is studded with square-cut stones rose-stones garnets
aquamarines and chrysolites and amethysts
Each stone is a chamber, a triangle pointing inward
along two sides are divans, the hypotenuse is the window
or a rectangle with three divans and a table in the middle

You can walk from room to room or take your ease
responding to color and your state of being. You can go
 all the way
You will still never get back. Your vision has changed.
I have been higher up—I could not see the heart
but saw the jewel on her breast like a rose-window
 shimmering
upon her breasts. Once I went higher up, once only:
into her Head. There was empty space. You floated in
                                        weightlessness.

English by Leif Sjöberg and Muriel Rukeyser
GUNNAR EKELÖF

THE LOST ROMANS

Where are they, not those young men, not those
                    young women
Who walked among the bullet-headed Romans with their
                    roads, their symmetry, their iron rule—
We know the dust and bones they are gone to, those
                    young Romans
Who stood against the bitter imperial, their young
                    green life with its poems—
Where are the poems made music against the purple
Setting their own purple up for a living sign,
Bright fire of some forgotten future against empire,
Their poems in the beautiful Roman tongue
Sex-songs, love-poems, freedom-songs?
Not only the young, but the old and in chains,
The slaves in their singing, the fierce northern
                    gentle blond rhythms,
The Judean cantillations, lullabies of Carthage,
Gaul with her cries, all the young Roman rebels,
Where are their songs?   Who will unlock them,
Who will find them for us, in some undiscovered
                    painted cave
For we need you, sisters, far brothers, poems
                    of our lost Rome.

CANAL

Sea-shouldering Ithaca
staring past sunset
after the islands
darkening closing
The narrow night. We
came in from Ithaca
into the inland
narrow water
trying to keep awake
while the ship went forward
but sleep came down
shouldering
down like Ithaca.
Night smites, light smites
and again light
in a narrow place
of old whiteness.
We are in
the narrowest place
moving in still
through an ash-white canal
a whitened plant
grappled to this wall
deep-cut, Judean slaves
cut the narrowest place
the ship fares into,

light smites again
the olive-plant in the crevice
captained through light.

FOR KAY BOYLE

What is the skill of this waking?   Heard the singing
of that man rambling up Frederick Street in music
and his repeated ecstasy, in a long shaken line.

After many and many a February storm, cyclamen
and many a curtain of rain, the tearing of all curtains
and, as you said, making love and facing the police

in one afternoon.   A few bright colors in permanent ink:
black sea, light like streetlight green, blue sees in you
the sun and the moon that stand as your guardians.

And the young bearded rebels and students tearing it all
    away,
all of it, down to the truth that barefaced naked act of
light, streamings of the courage of the sources,
the sun and the moon that stand at your ears.

RESURRECTION OF THE RIGHT SIDE

When the half-body dies its frightful death
forked pain, infection of snakes, lightning, pull down the
    voice. Waking
and I begin to climb the mountain on my mouth,
word by stammer, walk stammered, the lurching deck of
    earth.
Left-right with none of my own rhythms
the long-established sex and poetry.
                            I go running in sleep,
but waking stumble down corridors of self, all rhythms
    gone.

The broken movement of love   sex out of rhythm
one halted name   in a shattered language
ruin of French-blue lights behind the eyes
slowly the left hand extends a hundred feet
and the right hand follows follows
but still the power of sight is very weak
but I go rolling this ball of life, it rolls
and I follow it whole up the slowly-brightening slope

A whisper attempts me, I whisper without stammer
I walk the long hall to the time of a metronome
set by a child's gun-target   left-right

the power of eyesight is very slowly arriving
in this late impossible daybreak
all the blue flowers open

THE WARDS

St. George's Hospital, Hyde Park Corner

Lying in the moment, she climbs white snows;
At the foot of the bed the chart relates.
Here a man burns in fever; he is here, he is there,
Five thousand years ago in the cave country.
In this bed, I go wandering in Macao,
I run all night the black alleys. Time runs
Over the edge and all exists in all. We hold
All human history, all geography,
I cannot remember the word for what I need.
Our explorations, all at the precipice,
The night-table, a landscape of zebras,
Transistor constellations. All this music,
I heard it forming before I was born. I come
In this way, to the place.
                                Our selves lit clear,
This moment giving me necessity
Gives us ourselves and we risk everything,
Walking into our life.

THE SUN-ARTIST

for Bob Miller

I

The opening of the doors. Dark.
The opening of the large doors.
Out of the daylight and the scent of trees
and that lake where generations of swans
no longer move among children. In a poisoned time.
But the bright-headed children move.
Dark, high, the beams of a huge building
exposed in the high dark air.
I see brightness with a shock of joy.

II

Past the darkness a lashing of color.
Not color, strands of light.
Not light but pure deep color beyond color,
like the pure fierce light I once knew, before
a minute of blindness. These colors are deeper;
the entire range in its millions,
twisting and brilliant traveling.

III

I stand in the strong sun before a bank of prisms.
On the screen in front of me, tangled colors of light,
                              twined, intertwined.

A sensitive web of light changing, for the sun moves, the
   air moves.
The perceiver moves.
                         I dance my slow dance.

                         IV
The deepest blue, green, not the streams of the sea,
the clear yellow of tellows, not California, more,
not Mediterranean, not the Judean steeps.   Red beyond
                         blood over flame,
more even than visionary America.   All light.
A man braced on the sun, where the sun enters
through the roof, where the sun-follower,
a man-made motor with a gentle motion
just countered the movement of the earth, holds this scene
in front of us on the man-made screen.
Light traveling, meets, leaps and becomes art.

                         V
Colors move on a screen.   The doors open again.
They run in, the California children.
They run past the colors and the colors change.
The laughter of running.   They cry out, bird-voices,
ninety-seven children, Wow!   Wow!   How come?

                         VI
Another day.   I stand before the screen,
Alone I move, selecting out my green,
choose out the red with my arm, I let the orange stand,

a web of yellow, the blue stays and shines.
I am part of the color, I am part of the sun.

VII

You have made an art in which the sun is standing.
It changes, goes dark, goes grey.   The sun appears.
You have led me through eleven states of being.
You have invited us all.   Allow the sunlight,
dance your dance.

VIII

Another day.   No sun.   The fog is down,
Doing its slow dance into the city,
It enters the Gate and my waking.
There will be no colors but the range of white.
Before the screen,   I wait.

IX

Night.   What do you know about the light?

X

Waiting.   A good deal like real life.
Waiting before the sea for the fish to run
Waiting before the paper for the poem
Waiting for a man's life to be, to be.

XI

Break of light!   Sun in his colors,

streaming into our lives.

This artist dreams of the sun, the sun, the children of the
sun.

XII

Frail it is and can be intercepted.
Fragile, like ourselves.   Mirrors and prisms, they
                can be broken.
Children shattered by anything.
Strong, pouring strong, wild as the power of the great sun.
Not art, but light.   In distance, in smiting winter,
the artist speaks : No art.
This is not art.
What is *an artist?*   I bear the song of the sun.

POEM WHITE PAGE
WHITE PAGE POEM

Poem   white page   white page   poem
something is streaming out of a body in waves
something is beginning from the fingertips
they are starting to declare for my whole life
all the despair and the making music
something like wave after wave
that breaks on a beach
something like bringing the entire life
to this moment
the small waves bringing themselves to white paper
something like light stands up and is alive

FABLE

for Herbert Kohl

Yes it was the prince's kiss.
But the way was prepared for the prince.
It had to be.

When the attendants carrying the woman
—dead they thought her lying on the litter—
stumbled over the root of a tree
the bit of deathly apple in her throat
jolted free.

Not strangled, not poisoned!
She
can come alive.

It was an "accident" they hardly noticed.

The threshold here comes when they stumble.
The jolt.   And better if we notice,
However, their noticing is not
Essential to the story.

A miracle has even deeper roots,
Something like error, some profound defeat.
Stumbled-over, the startle, the arousal,
Something never perceived till now, the taproot.

NERUDA, THE WINE

We are the seas through whom the great fish passed
And passes. He died in a moment of general dying.
Something was reborn. What was it, Pablo?
Something is being reborn : poems, death, ourselves,
The link deep in our peoples, the dead link in our dead
     regimes,
The last of our encounters transformed from the first
Long ago in Xavier's house, where you lay sick,
Speaking of poems, the sheet pushed away
Growth of beard pressing up, fierce grass, as you spoke.
And that last moment in the hall of students,
Speaking at last of Spain, that core of all our lives,
The long defeat that brings us what we know.
Meaning, poems, lifelong in loss and presence passing for-
     ever.
I spilled the wine at the table
And you, Pablo, dipped your finger in it and marked my
     forehead.
Words, blood, rivers, cities, days.   I go, a woman signed
     by you—
The poems of the wine.

BEFORE DANGER

There were poems all over Broadway that morning.
Blowing across traffic.   Against the legs.
Held for a moment on the backs of hands.
Drifts of poems in doorways.
The crowd was a river to the highest tower
all the way down that avenue.
Snow on that river, torn paper
of their faces.

Late at night, in a dark-blue sleep,
the paper stopped blowing.
Lightning struck at me from behind my eyes.

SONG : REMEMBERING MOVIES

remembering movies   love
remembering songs
remembering the scenes and flashes of your life
given to me as we lay dreaming
giving dreams
in the sharp flashes of light
raining from the scenes of your life
the faithless stories, adventures, discovery
sexuality opening range after range
and the sharp music driven forever into my life
I sing the movies of your life
the sequences cut in rhythms of collision
rhythms of linkage, love,
I sing the songs

WORK, FOR THE DAY IS COMING

It is the poem, yes
that it exist   that it grow in reach
that it grow into lives not yet born not yet speaking.
That its sounds move with the grace of meaning
the liquid sharing, the abrupt clash of lives.
That its suggestions climb to
     descend to   the fire of finding
          the last breath of the poem
              and further.
For that I move through states of being,
the struggle to wake, the frightful morning,
the flash of ecstacy among our mutilations,
the recognizing light   shining   and all night long
am invited led whipped dragged through states of being
toward the
          inviting you through states of being

                    poem.

RECOVERING

Dream of the world
speaking to me.

The dream of the dead
acted out in me.

The fathers shouting
across their blue gulf.

A storm in each word,
an incomplete universe.

Lightning in brain,
slow-time recovery.

In the light of October
things emerge clear.

The force of looking
returns to my eyes.

Darkness arrives
splitting the mind open.

Something again

is beginning to be born.

A dance is
dancing me.

I wake in the dark.

PARALLEL INVENTION

We in our season like progress and inventions.
The inventor is really the invention.
But who made the inventions? To what uses
Were they put, by whom, and for what purposes?

You made an innovation and then
did you give it to me without writing it down?
Did you give it to her, too?
Did I develop it and give it to him,
or to her, or to them?

Did you quicken communication,
Did you central-control? And war? And the soul?

Let's not talk about communication
any more.

Did we deepen our integration ties
did we subsequently grow—
in strength? in complexity?

Or did we think of doing the same things
at the same time and do them to each other?

And then out of our lovemaking
emergence of priests and kings,

out of our smiles and twists
full-time craft specialists,
out of our mouths and asses
division into social classes,
art and architecture and writing
from meditation and delighting
from our terrors and our pities
"of course," you say, "the growth of cities."

But parallels do not imply
identities—there is no iron law;
we are richly variable
levels of heaven and levels of hell;
ripples of change out from the center
of me, of you, of love the inventor.

After reading an essay by Robert McC. Adams in *Civilization**
—found in the Women's Detention Center, Washington—D.C.D.C.

* Edited by Williams *et al.* 6th edition. Published by Scott Fores-
man, 1969.

POEM

Green going through the jungle of those years
I see the brilliant bodies of the invaders
And the birds cry in the high trees, the sky
Flashes above me in bright crevices; time is,
And I go on and the birds fly blurred
And I pass, my eyes seeing through corpses of dead cells
Glassy, a world hardening with my hardening eyes
My look is through the corpses of all the living
Men and women who stood with me and died before
But my young look still blazes from my changing
Eyes and the jungle asserts fiery green
Even though the trees are the trees of home
And we look out of eyes filled with dead cells
See through these hours, faces of what we are.

NOT TO BE PRINTED,
NOT TO BE SAID,
NOT TO BE THOUGHT

I'd rather be Muriel
than be dead and be Ariel.

BACK TOOTH

My large back tooth, without a mate for years,
at last has been given one. The dentist ground her down
a bit. She had been growing wild, nothing to meet her,
   keep her sane.
Now she fits the new one, they work together, sleep to-
   gether,
she is a little diminished but functioning, all night all day.

DESTRUCTION OF GRIEF

Today I asked Aileen
at the Film Library to help me find
those girl twins of the long-gone summer.
Aileen, who were they?
I was seven, the lion circus
was pitched in the field of sand and swordgrass
near the ocean, behind the Tackapoosha Garage.
The ancient land of the Waramaug Indians.
Now there's a summer hotel.
The first day of that circus dazzles me forever.
I stayed.   That evening
the police came looking for me.
Easy to find, behind
the bales of hay, with Caesar's tamer,
the clowns, and the girl twins.
My father and mother forgave me, for they loved
circuses, opera, carnivals, New York, popular songs.
All day that summer, all July and August,
I stayed behind the tents with the twin girls,
with Caesar the lion my friend,
with the lion-tamer.
Do you know their names, Aileen?
The girls went into the early movies.
Late August, Caesar mauled the man's right hand.
I want to remember the names of those twins.
You could see he would not ever keep his hand.

Smell of the ocean, straw,
lordly animal rankness, gunpowder.
"Yes, they destroyed Caesar," I was told that night.
Those twins became movie stars.
Those of us who were there that summer—
Joey killed himself, I saw Tommy
just before the war; is Henry around?
Helene is in real estate—and the twins—
can you tell me their names, Aileen?

TRINITY CHURCHYARD

for my mother & her ancestor, Akiba

Wherever I walked I went green among young growing
Along the same song, Mother, even along this grass
Where, Mother, tombstones stand each in its pail of shade
In Trinity yard where you at lunchtime came
As a young workingwoman, Mother, bunches of your
    days, grapes
Pressing your life into mine, Mother,
And I never cared for these tombs and graves
But they are your book-keeper hours.

You said to me summers later, deep in your shiniest car
As a different woman, Mother, and I your poem-making
    daughter—
"Each evening after I worked all day for the lock-people
"I wished under a green sky on the young evening star—
"What did I wish for?" What did you wish for, Mother?
"I wished for a man, of course, anywhere in my world,
"And there was Trinity graveyard and the tall New York
    steeples."

Wherever I go, Mother, I stay away from graves
But they turn everywhere in the turning world; now,
Mother Rachel's, on the road from Jerusalem.
And mine is somewhere turning unprepared
In the earth or among the whirling air.
My workingwoman mother is saying to me, Girl—

Years before her rich needy unreal years—
Whatever work you do, always make sure
You can go walking, not like me, shut in your hours.

Mother I walk, going even here in green Galilee
Where our ancestor, Akiba, resisted Rome,
Singing forever for the Song of Songs
Even in torture knowing.   Mother, I walk, this blue,
The Sea, Mother, this hillside, to his great white stone.
And again here in New York later I come alone
To you, Mother, I walk, making our poems.

BURNISHING, OAKLAND

Near the waterfront
mouth of a wide shed   open
many-shining bronze flat
ship-propellors hanging in air
propellors lying blunt on ground
The vast sound and shine
screaming its word

One man masked
holding a heavy weight
on the end of a weighted boom
counterbalanced
I see him draw
his burnisher
along the bronze
high scream of burnishing
a path of brightness

Outside, the prowl cars
Oakland police
cruising past
behind them the trailing
Panther cars
to witness to

any encounter

Statement of light
I see as we drive past
act of light
among sleeping houses
in our need
the dark people

Behind my head
the shoulders of hills
and the dark houses.
Here the shine, the singing cry
near the extreme
of the range of knowing
one masked man
working alone
burnishing

THE IRIS-EATERS

for John Cage

It was like everything else, like everything—
nothing at all like what they say it is.
The petals of iris were slightly cinnamon,
a smooth beard in the mouth
transforming to strong drink,
light violet turning purple in the throat
and flashed and went deep red
burning and burning.
Well, no, more an extreme warmth,
but we thought of burning,
we thought of poisons,
we thought of the closing of the throat
forever, of dying, of the end of song.
We were doing it, you understand,
for the first time.
You were the only one of us who knew
and you saved us, John,
with music, with a
                    complex
                              smile.

SLOW DEATH OF THE DRAGON

The sickness poured through the roads,
The vineyards shook.
A clot formed on the wild river.
The streets and squares were full of crevices.
Poison ran on the church-towers.
The olive trees!
He shook for thirty years,
Held his buttocks tense while his varnished officers
Broke thighs, broke fingers.
A man dies.
The genitals of the South are broken.
Venom pours
Into his provinces of pain.

The surgeons come.
Are there children left alive
Among his bones?   The drugs of choice are used,
Sleep-poison, torture-dream-drink, elixir of silence,
Rousing of memory : the inquisition.
Purgation of the future. "Cut off this lobe," they said.
"The heart is rejecting the present."   On the roads
The dead of the resistance tried to stand
Again, they tried to stand again.
But they were dead.

The surgeons are cutting out his words.
Too late; all the children are silent.

On the central plateau, snow is falling.
Incisions split the open country.   On the coast of pain,
All craft becalmed.   The surgeons are singing.
No, of course the dragon is not dead.
A branch of a tree is dead.
A generation is dead.
Most of the living are silent.
Prepare the ink on the rollers;
This has been a long time coming.
The posters carry one word:
Today!

Send the word underground, where water flows,
Clear, pure, black.
Is it beyond taint?
No, it is not beyond taint.
Certain women and men look at us out of their eyes.
Do they begin to speak
They have been speaking all along.
We can tell by their eyes,
Although their mouths are broken.
Now they are healing their mouths;
They have been speaking during all this dead lifetime.
Has the dragon died?
Something is beginning to be born,
But the seeds of the dragon are also growing in the fresh
     wombs of girls.
O love.   Make the song start.

Summer 1936—Winter 1975

MENDINGS

for Alfred Marshak

You made healing as you wanted us to make bread and
 poems.
In your abrasive life of gifts,
In the little ravine telling the life of the future
When your science would be given to all,
A broken smile.
In the sun, speaking of the joining of nerve-endings,
Make the wounds part of the well body.
Make a healed life.
You shouted, waving your hand with the last phalange
Of the little finger missing, you whole man,
"Make it well! Make things accessible!"
He is a pollinating man. We are his seedlings.
Marshak, I was your broken nerve-endings,
You made your man-made bridges over the broken nerves.
What did you do? Inspect potatoes, wait for passports,
 do your research,
While the State Department lady was saying, "Let him
 swim,"
While the chief who had the power to allow your uses
To move, a proper use of plastic, a bridge across broken
 nerves
Stopped you there (and asked me to marry him).
Saying to you, Marshak, full of creation as the time
Went deeper into war, and you to death:
"The war will be over before your work is ready."

THEN

When I am dead, even then,
I will still love you, I will wait in these poems,
When I am dead, even then
I am still listening to you.
I will still be making poems for you
out of silence;
silence will be falling into that silence,
it is building music.

TWO

Scaffolding. *A poet is in solitary; the expectation is that he will be tried and summarily executed on a certain day in autumn. He has been on this cycle before : condemned to death, the sentence changed to life imprisonment, and then a pardon from his President during a time of many arrests and executions, a time of terror. The poet has written his stinging work—like that of Burns or Brecht— and it has got under the skin of the highest officials.*

An American woman is sent to make an appeal for the poet's life. She speaks to Cabinet ministers, the Cardinal, university people, writers, the poet's family and his infant son. She stands in the mud and rain at the prison gates— also the gates of perception, the gates of the body. She is before the house of the poet. He is in solitary.

Waiting to leave all day I hear the words;
That poet in prison, that poet newly-died
whose words we wear, reading, all of us.   I and my son.

All day we read the words:
friends, lovers, daughters, grandson,
and all night the distant loves
and I who had never seen him am drawn to him

Through acts, through poems,
through our closenesses—
whatever links us in our variousness;
across worlds, love and poems and justices
wishing to be born.

Walking the world to find the poet of these cries.
But this walking is flying the streets of all the air.

Walking the world, through the people at airports,
this city of hills, this island ocean fire-blue and now this
    city.

Walking this world is driving the roads of houses
endless tiles   houses, fast streams, now this child's house.

Walking under the sharp mountains through the sharp
    city
circled in time by rulers, their grip; the marvelous
hard-gripped people silent among their rulers, looking
    at me.

The new friend comes into my hotel room
smiling.   He does a curious thing.
He walks around the room, touching
all the pictures hanging on the wall.
One picture does not move.

A new friend assures me   :   Foreigners are safe,
You speak for writers, you are safe, he says.
There will be no car
driving up behind you, there will be
no accident, he says.   I know these accidents.
Nothing will follow you, he says.
O the Mafia at home, I know, Black Hand
of childhood, the death of Tresca whom I mourn,
the building of New York.   Many I know.
This morning I go early to see the Cardinal.
When I return, the new friend is waiting.   His face
wax-candle-pool-color, he saying
"I thought you were kidnapped."

A missionary comes to visit me.
Looks into my eyes.   Says,
"Turn on the music so we can talk."

4

The Cabinet minister speaks of liberation.
"Do you know how the Communists use this word?"
We all use the word.   Liberation.

No, but look—these are his diaries,
says the Cabinet minister.
These were found in the house of the poet.
Look, Liberation, Liberation, he is speaking in praise.

He says, this poet, It is not wrong
to take from the rich and give to the poor.

Yes.   He says it in prose speech, he says it in his plays,
he says it in his poems that bind me to him,
that bind his people and mine in these new ways
for the first time past strangeness and despisal.

It also means that you broke into his house and stole his
    papers.

5

Among the days,
among the nights of the poet in solitary,
a strong infant is just beginning to run.
I go up the stepping-stones
to where the young wife of the poet
stands holding the infant in her arms.
She weeps, she weeps.
But the poet's son looks at me
and the wife's mother looks at me with a keen look
across her grief.   Lights in the house, books making every
    wall
a wall of speech.
                    The clasp of the woman's hand
around my wrist, a keen band
more steel than the words
Save his life.

I feel that clasp on my bones.

A strong infant is beginning to run.

As we climb to the church of Galilee
Three harsh men on the corner.
As we go to the worship-meeting of the dismissed,
three state police on the street.
As we all join at the place of the dispossessed,
three dark men asking their rote questions.
As we go ahead to stand with our new friends
that will be our friends our lifetime.
Introduced as dismissed from this faculty, this college,
this faculty, this university.
'Dismissed' is now an honorary degree.
The harsh police are everywhere,
they have hunted this fellowship away before
and they are everywhere, at the street-corner,
listening to all hymns,
standing before all doors,
hearing over all wires.
We go up to Galilee.
Let them listen to the dispossessed
and to all women and men who stand firm and sing
wanting a shared and honest lifetime.
Let them listen to Galilee.

That night, a flute
across the dark, the sound
opening times to me, a time
when I stood on the green hillside
before the great white stone.
Grave of my ancestor
Akiba at rest over Kinneret.
The holy poem, he said to me,
the Song of Songs always;
and know what I know, to love
your belief with all your life,
and resist the Romans, as I did,
even to the torture and beyond.
Over Kinneret, with all of them,
Jesus, all the Judeans,
that other Galilee
in dream across war I see.

Woman seen as a slender instrument,
woman at vigil in the prison-yard,
woman seen as the fine tines of a pitchfork
that works hard, that is worn down, rusted down
to a fine sculpture standing in a yard
where her son's body is confined.
Woman as fine tines blazing against sunset,
wavering lines against yellow brightness
where her fine body becomes transparent in bravery,
where she will live and die as the tines of a pitchfork
that stands to us as her son's voice does stand
across the world speaking

The rumor comes that if this son is killed
this mother will kill herself

But she is here, she lives,
the slender tines of this pitchfork standing in flames of
    light.

·9·

You grief woman   you gave me a scarlet coverlet
thick-sown with all the flowers
and all the while your poet sleeps in stone

Grief woman, the waves of this coverlet,
roses of Asia,
they flicker soft and bright over my sleep

all night while the poet waits in solitary

All you vigil women, I start up in the night,
fling back this cover of red;
in long despair we work   write   speak   pray   call to others
Free our night   free our lives   free our poet

10

Air fills with fear and the kinds of fear:

The fear of the child among the tyrannical
unanswerable men and women, they dominate day and
   night.

Fear of the young lover in the huge rejection
ambush of sex and of imagination;
fear that the world will not allow your work.

Fear of the overarching wars and poverties,
the terrible exiles,
all bound by corruption until at last! we speak!

And those at home in jail who protest the frightful war
and the beginning : The woman-guard says to me, Spread
   your cheeks,
the search begins and I begin to know.

And also at home the nameless multitude
of fears : fear in childbirth for the living child,
fear for the child deformed and loved, fear
among the surgeries that can cure her, fear
for the child's father, and for oneself, fear.
Fear of the cunt and cock in their terrible powers
and here a world away fear of the jailers' tortures

for we invent our fear and act it out
in ripping, in burning, in blood, in the terrible scream
and in tearing away every mouth that screams.

Giant fears : massacres, the butchered that across the fields
    of the world
lie screaming, and their screams are heard as silence.
O love, knowing your love across a world of fear,
I lie in a strange country, in pale yellow, swamp-green,
    woods
and a night of music while a poet lies in solitary
somewhere in a concrete cell. Glare-lit, I hear,
without books, without pen and paper.
Does he draw a pencil out of his throat,
out of his veins, out of his sex?
There are cells all around him, emptied.
He can signal on these walls till he runs mad.
He is signalling to me across the night.

He is signalling. Many of us speak,
we do teach each other, we do act through our fears.

Where is the world that will touch life to this prison?

We run through the night. We are given his gifts.

11

Long ago, soon after my son's birth
– this scene comes in arousal with the sight of a strong
    child
just beginning to run –
when all life seemed prisoned off, because the father's
    other son
born three weeks before my child
had opened the world
that other son and his father closed the world –
in my fierce loneliness and fine well-being
torn apart but with my amazing child
I celebrated and grieved.
And before that baby
had ever started to begin to run
then Mary said,
smiling and looking out of her Irish eyes,
"Never mind, Muriel.
Life will come will come again
knocking and coughing and farting at your door."

12

For that I cannot name the names,
my child's own father, the flashing, the horseman,
the son of the poet—
for that he never told me another child was started,
to come to birth three weeks before my own.
Tragic timing that sets the hands of time.
O wind from our own coast, turning
around the turning world.

Wind from the continents, this other child,
child of this moment and this moment's poet.
Again I am struck nameless, unable to name,
and the axe-blows fall heavy heavy and sharp
and the moon strikes his white light down over the
    continents
on this strong infant and the heroic friends
silent in this terrifying moment under all moonlight,
all sunlight turning in all our unfree lands.
Name them, name them all, light of our own time.

13

Crucified child—is he crucified?   he is tortured,
kept away from his father, spiked on time,
crucified we say, cut off from the man
they want to kill—
he runs toward me in Asia, crying.
Flash gives me my own son strong and those years ago
cut off from his own father and running toward me
holding a strong flower.

Child of this moment, you are your father's child
wherever your father is prisoned, by what tyrannies
or jailed as my child's father
by his own fantasies—
child of the age running among the world,
standing among us who carry our own time.

14

So I became very dark very large
a silent woman this time given to speech
a woman of the river   of that song
and on the beach of the world in storm given
in long lightning seeing the rhyming of those scenes
that make our lives.
Anne Sexton the poet saying
ten days ago to that receptive friend,
the friend of the hand-held camera:
"Muriel is serene."
Am I that in their sight?
Word comes today of Anne's
of Anne's long-approaching
of Anne's over-riding over-falling
suicide. Speak for   sing for   pray for
everyone in solitary
every living life.

15

All day the rain
all day waiting within the prison gate
before another prison gate
The house of the poet
He is in there somewhere
among the muscular wardens
I have arrived at the house of the poet
in the mud in the interior music of all poems
and the grey rain of the world
whose gates do not open.
I stand, and for this religion and that religion
do not eat but remember all the things I know
and a strong infant beginning to run.
Nothing is happening.   Mud, silence, rain.

Near the end of the day
with the rain and the knowledge pulling at my legs
a movement behind me makes me move aside.
A bus full of people turns in the mud, drives to the gate.
The gate that never opens
opens at last.   Beyond it, slender
Chinese-red posts of the inner gates.
The gate of the house of the poet.

The bus is crowded, a rush-hour bus that waits.

Nobody moves.

"Who are these people?" I say.
How can these gates open?

My new friend has run up beside me.
He has been standing guard in the far corner.
"They are prisoners," he says, "brought here from trial.
Don't you see? They are all tied together."

Fool that I am! I had not seen the ropes,
down at their wrists in the crowded rush-hour bus.

The gates are open.   The prisoners go in.
The house of the poet who stays in solitary,
not allowed reading   not allowed writing
not allowed   his woman   his friends   his unknown
        friends
and the strong infant beginning to run.

We go down the prison hill.   On our right, sheds
full of people all leaning forward, blown on some ferry.
"They are the families of the prisoners.   Some can visit.
They are waiting for their numbers to be called."

How shall we venture home?
How shall we tell each other of the poet?
How can we meet the judgment on the poet,

or his execution?   How shall we free him?
How shall we speak to the infant beginning to run?
All those beginning to run?